1&2 KINGS

GOD'S IMPERFECT SERVANTS

CAROLYN
NYSTROM

10 STUDIES
FOR INDIVIDUALS
OR GROUPS

Life
Builder
Study

INTER-VARSITY PRESS
36 Causton Street, London SW1P 4ST, England
Email: ivp@ivpbooks.com
Website: www.ivpbooks.com

Originally published in the United States of America as Characters and Kings: Woman's
Workshop on the History of Israel, Parts I and II *in 1985 by Zondervan, Grand Rapids,
Minnesota*
Second edition published as Old Testament Kings *in 1993 by InterVarsity Press, Downers
Grove, Illinois*
Third edition published as 1 & 2 Kings *in the LifeGuide® Bible Studies series in 2018*
First published in Great Britain in 2018

British Library Cataloguing-in-Publication Data
A catalogue record for this book is available from the British Library.

ISBN: 978–1–78359–675–1
eBook ISBN: 978–1–78359–676–8

Printed in Great Britain by Ashford Colour Press Ltd, Gosport, Hampshire

*Inter-Varsity Press publishes Christian books that are true to the Bible and that communicate
the gospel, develop discipleship and strengthen the church for its mission in the world.*

*IVP originated within the Inter-Varsity Fellowship, now the Universities and Colleges Christian
Fellowship, a student movement connecting Christian Unions in universities and colleges
throughout Great Britain, and a member movement of the International Fellowship of
Evangelical Students. Website: www.uccf.org.uk. That historic association is maintained,
and all senior IVP staff and committee members subscribe to the UCCF Basis of Faith.*

Contents

Getting the Most Out of
1 & 2 Kings

What good will it do twenty-first century Christians to study kings who ruled a nation of Hebrews three thousand years ago? For people who get excited about battles and dates and ancient political maneuverings, the answer is obvious. All history, even Hebrew history, is great.

But what about the rest of us? God must have had some reason for designing his Holy Book so that one-third of the Old Testament text recounts historical events. He wasn't just entertaining history buffs. A look at the issues surrounding these kings will give us some clues.

We see Solomon, who prayed as if he knew exactly what God desired to give, then fell into paganism under the influence of his seven hundred (!) wives. And we ask, "Do *I* ever place the people I love ahead of God?"

We see Jeroboam and Rehoboam, who split their nation in civil war and then split their places of worship. Who among us has endured civil war within our church that could end in separate places of worship?

We see Ahaz who, when faced with trouble, stopped believing in God. And we wonder about our own ability to keep faith in the face of despair.

We see Hoshea who angered God so much by his determination to serve other gods that God terminated his nation. And we pray for our own national leaders, and thereby for ourselves.

We see Manasseh, the most wicked king of all. Yet God let him reign for forty-five years, the longest reign of any Hebrew king. We wonder how our faith, rattled by an afternoon of inconvenience, would endure an era when the king killed God worshipers every day.

We see Josiah, who became a king at the age of eight yet turned his nation to worship God. And we wonder about our influence for God on our own children—and the results of their influence on others.

We see Zedekiah, the last Hebrew king, presiding over a nation already dead, and we look for hope from a God who is not stopped by death.

They ruled for four centuries, these Hebrew kings. There were forty-two of them. Some ruled only days, others for a lifetime. Some were so minor that they rate only a line of text, others fill whole books. Some were evil; some were good. The biblical text evaluates each one at the end of his life—a reminder that we, ourselves, will undergo the same evaluation.

But when the narrative of the kings ends with the fall of Judah in 587 BC, their names are not forgotten. In the opening pages of the New Testament, they live again. It seems that when God chose a family for his Son, the infant Jesus, he chose from a line of kings. When we read Joseph's genealogy, we find, among all those hard-to-pronounce names, a familiar line: the kings of Israel.

Let us read from them and learn. None was perfect, and neither are we. But God was sovereign—even over the kings. And he is sovereign over us as well.

Suggestions for Individual Study

1. As you begin each study, pray that God will speak to you through his Word.

2. Read the introduction to the study and respond to the personal reflection question or exercise. This is designed to help you focus on God and on the theme of the study.

3. Each study deals with a particular passage so that you can delve into the author's meaning in that context. Read and reread the passage to be studied. The questions are written using the language of the New International Version, so you may wish to use that version of the Bible. The New Revised Standard Version is also recommended.

4. This is an inductive Bible study, designed to help you discover for yourself what Scripture is saying. The study includes three types of questions. *Observation* questions ask about the basic facts: who, what, when, where, and how. *Interpretation* questions delve into the meaning of the passage. *Application* questions help you discover the implications of the text for growing in Christ. These three keys unlock the treasures of Scripture.

Write your answers to the questions in the spaces provided or in a personal journal. Writing can bring clarity and deeper understanding of yourself and of God's Word.

5. It might be good to have a Bible dictionary handy. Use it to look up any unfamiliar words, names, or places.

6. Use the prayer suggestion to guide you in thanking God for what you have learned and to pray about the applications that have come to mind.

7. You may want to go on to the suggestion under "Now or Later," or you may want to use that idea for your next study.

Suggestions for Members of a Group Study

1. Come to the study prepared. Follow the suggestions for individual study mentioned above. You will find that careful preparation will greatly enrich your time spent in group discussion.

2. Be willing to participate in the discussion. The leader of your group will not be lecturing. Instead, he or she will be encouraging the members of the group to discuss what they have learned. The leader will be asking the questions that are found in this guide.

3. Stick to the topic being discussed. Your answers should be based on the verses that are the focus of the discussion and not on outside authorities such as commentaries or speakers. These studies focus on a particular passage of Scripture. Only rarely should you refer to other portions of the Bible. This allows for everyone to participate in in-depth study on equal ground.

4. Be sensitive to the other members of the group. Listen attentively when they describe what they have learned. You may be surprised by their insights! Each question assumes a variety of answers. Many questions do not have "right" answers, particularly questions that aim at meaning or application. Instead the questions push us to explore the passage more thoroughly.

When possible, link what you say to the comments of others. Also, be affirming whenever you can. This will encourage some of the more hesitant members of the group to participate.

5. Be careful not to dominate the discussion. We are sometimes so eager to express our thoughts that we leave too little opportunity for others to respond. By all means participate! But allow others to also.

6. Expect God to teach you through the passage being discussed and through the other members of the group. Pray that you will have an enjoyable and profitable time together, but also that as a result of the study you will find ways that you can take action individually and/or as a group.

7. Remember that anything said in the group is considered confidential and should not be discussed outside the group unless specific permission is given to do so.

8. If you are the group leader, you will find additional suggestions at the back of the guide.

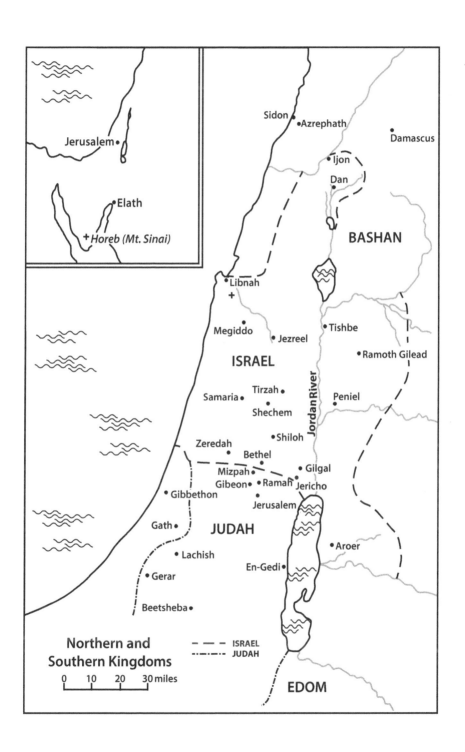

Sidon
•Azrephath
•Damascus
Jerusalem•

Elath
+ Horeb (Mt. Sinai)

•Ijon
Dan•

BASHAN

•Libnah
+
Megiddo•
•Jezreel
•Tishbe

ISRAEL
•Ramoth Gilead

Samaria•
Tirzah•
Shechem•
Peniel•

Jordan River

•Shiloh

Zeredah•
Bethel•
•Gilgal
Mizpah•
Gibeon•
•Ramah
Jericho
Gibbethon•
Jerusalem•

Gath•
JUDAH
•Aroer

•Lachish
En-Gedi•
•Gerar

Beetsheba•

Northern and
Southern Kingdoms

– – – ISRAEL
–·–·– JUDAH

0   10   20   30 miles

EDOM

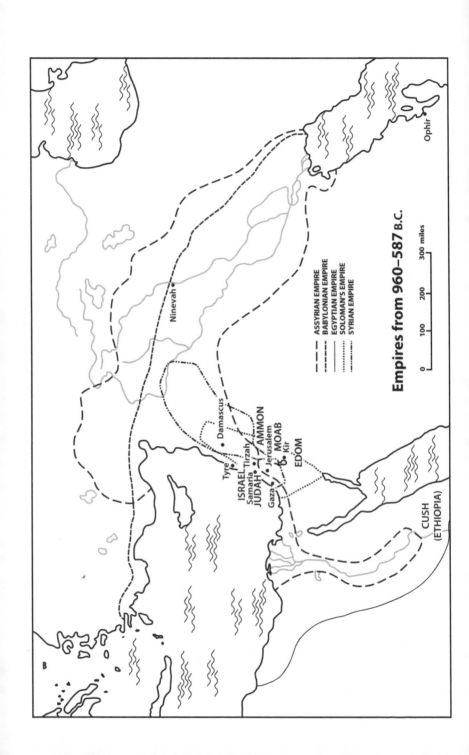

Empires from 960–587 B.C.

ASSYRIAN EMPIRE -- -- --
BABYLONIAN EMPIRE -- -- --
EGYPTIAN EMPIRE ———
SOLOMAN'S EMPIRE ·········
SYRIAN EMPIRE -··-··-

0   100   200   300 miles

Ophir

Ninevah

Damascus
Tyre
ISRAEL
Samaria Tirzah
JUDAH   AMMON
Gaza Jerusalem
MOAB
Kir
EDOM

CUSH
(ETHIOPIA)

1

Solomon

Praying with God's Values

1 Kings 3

"Hello, Mary? I need a listening ear. Do you have time?"

Haltingly, I poured out my disappointment and sorrow about a problem that had been plaguing me for days. Mary made sympathetic noises, offered a few corrective comments, and promised to pray. The situation went unchanged. Yet, as the day progressed, I felt the cloud of sadness lift. I knew Mary was praying. And God, in his generosity, was granting the requests of her prayer.

Why had I chosen Mary—because she was approachable? Partly. But more because I knew her spiritual walk. It was carefully metered by Christlike patterns. And because she was comfortable with prayer, her prayers were specific and to the point. Like her spiritual walk, her prayers seemed closely matched to God's values.

GROUP DISCUSSION. If you wanted someone to pray for you, who would you call? Why would you choose that person?

PERSONAL REFLECTION. Take a quick mental assessment of your current practice of prayer. How would you grade yourself: A, B, C, or D? Why?

The first day of school, the first line of a sermon, the first page of a book—first impressions are important. *Read 1 Kings 3:1-15.*

1. What were some of Solomon's actions in the early years of his reign (vv. 1-5)?

If you had been in Solomon's sandals, what might you be thinking or asking at this point?

2. What do Solomon's actions in this setting suggest about his character?

3. Solomon answered God's question with a prayer (vv. 6-9). What does Solomon's prayer suggest about his attitude toward himself, his job, and his God?

4. What did God promise Solomon (vv. 10-15)?

5. What conditions did God attach to granting Solomon a long life?

6. How would you describe a discerning heart (or mind)?

7. Think of one of your current responsibilities that seems a bit too large for you. What would you *like* to ask of God in that area?

_____

8. What *should* you ask of God?

_____

9. *Read 1 Kings 3:16-28.* Imagine yourself as a bystander in King Solomon's court. What emotions would you feel during the different stages of the hearing?

_____

10. Do you agree that Solomon's method of judgment was wise? Why or why not?

_____

11. In what specific ways did God answer Solomon's prayer of verses 7-9?

_____

12. How might you begin to bring your prayers more into line with God's values?

Think of one person who particularly needs a discerning mind right now. Pray one or two sentences asking God's help for that person.

Now or Later

Before God, consider one of your own responsibilities that seems beyond your capability, and ask God for "a wise and discerning heart."

2

Solomon

Faithless in Love

1 Kings 11

It's an old and cruel trick used by ruthless conquering nations for millennia: Kill the young men. Marry the young women. Then the next generation (the children) will become loyal to their conquerors. Israel's King Solomon created his own version of this brutal practice. But it cost him—and his nation.

GROUP DISCUSSION. Describe one marriage in which you have seen faith and love work well together.

PERSONAL REFLECTION. What sometimes tempts you to less than wholehearted commitment to God?

Some of God's laws may seem harsh, but they are less harsh than the results of living by our own guidelines. God seems to know what works. King Solomon had occasion to discover this truth because Solomon loved women—lots of them. *Read 1 Kings 11:1-25.*

1. What negative effects did wealth and power have on Solomon?

2. Why had God commanded his people not to intermarry with the nations around them (v. 2)?

---

3. In what ways did Solomon break the first commandment, "You shall have no other gods before me" (vv. 1-13)?

---

4. In verse 13 God says that the consequence of Solomon's sin is that his kingdom will be taken away. What mercy does God promise? Why?

---

5. Solomon allowed his acquisition of wives to dilute his faith in God. When has your own affection for a person created tensions with your faith?

---

6. How can we balance our love for the important people in our lives with our love for God?

---

7. What indications do you see that Hadad had the potential to become a serious threat to Solomon (vv. 14-22)?

What about Rezon (vv. 23-25)?

8. *Read 1 Kings 11:26-43.* How did God use Ahijah's new cloak as a message to Jeroboam (vv. 29-31)?

_____

9. If Jeroboam had chosen to benefit from the experience of Israel's previous two kings, how might it have affected his reign?

_____

10. Verse 6 characterizes Solomon's life with the words, "Solomon did evil in the eyes of the LORD." Why do you think God described such a successful king in this way?

_____

11. Solomon's marriages to women who served other gods testified to his lack of wholehearted commitment to the one true God. What influences in your life test your ability to keep your actions in line with your beliefs?

Take a few moments of silence inviting God to bring to your mind what most tempts you away from a God-first life. To the extent that you are able, ask God to refocus your mind and heart toward his priorities.

Now or Later

Do a little checking into your heritage from your family tree: eyes, hair, body shape. Consider also your spiritual heritage: belief systems, hardships, cultural values, challenges, church relationships.

Thank God for the strengths and talents you find there. Take note of any flaws you might want to overcome if they happen to appear in your own life.

3

Jeroboam
and Rehoboam

1 Kings 12

Civil war. American minds turn to Yankee blue battling Confederate gray; brothers, cousins, and neighbors pitted against each other; a wantonly destructive march to the sea—forever an embarrassment to both sides; a president on his knees in tears.

Three thousand years ago, Israel too suffered civil war with many of the same griefs. As in the US Civil War, family members had to decide which side they were on. However, for the people of Israel, geography wasn't always the most important factor. This war was not only a war of politics—it was also, at least at the outset, a war of faith.

GROUP DISCUSSION. How do you respond to conflict within your church or fellowship group?

PERSONAL REFLECTION. How does that kind of conflict affect your faith?

There are many ways to divide a country. This study's Scripture tells us of a Hebrew version of civil war. *Read 1 Kings 12:1-24.*

1. What steps in these verses led to the division recorded in verse 20?

2. At what points did reconciliation seem possible?

3. What volatile words and actions on both sides fanned the disagreement into open war (vv. 10-16)?

4. Verse 8 tells us that Rehoboam "rejected the advice the elders gave him and consulted the young men who had grown up with him." When and how have you come to value the wisdom or experience of someone who is not your age?

5. What indications do you find that God had not abandoned his people even during this time of conflict?

6. If you had to go through a civil war, of what value would it be for you to know that nothing is outside the power of God?

---

7. *Read 1 Kings 12:25-33.* Looking at the map on page **9**, what geographic reasons can you see for Jeroboam's selection of these sites?

---

8. What motivated Jeroboam to set up alternate places of worship (vv. 26-27)?

---

9. What spiritual results for the people of Israel would you expect to grow out of Jeroboam's new places of worship?

---

10. What did Jeroboam do that was contrary to God's law for his people? (Find all that you can in verses 31-33.)

11. If you were a godly person living under Jeroboam's rule, what choices would you have to make?

_____

12. In what ways have you taken for granted your current opportunities to worship?

_____

13. What steps could you take to worship God more fully?

Pray for your own church. Ask God for spiritual health and unity.

Now or Later

Create a list of seven people who have some form of responsibility in your church. Pray for one of them each day of the coming week.

4

Ahab

A commuter poking the buttons of a car radio catches a few words from a British preacher and quickly moves on. A child sitting in an animated Sunday school class picks at a thread on her skirt, eyes aimed at the floor.

We each have our own methods of tuning out God. For example, singing an entire hymn without a single word registering in the mind, meticulously compiling a to-do list during the sermon, accidentally leaving a Bible at church and not missing it for days, feeling no compunction about a pattern of daily prayer long since abandoned and hardly remembered.

GROUP DISCUSSION. "Don't nobody bring me no bad news" sings witch Glinda in the 1978 musical *The Wiz*, created by Charlie Smalls. When have you said (or wished) something similar?

PERSONAL REFLECTION. What do you do, or not do, that sometimes makes you deaf to God?

There are many paths by which we can become deaf to God. Ahab's life (and death) warns us against such a route. *Read 1 Kings 22:1-28.*

1. List all the characters in this drama. How is each person important in this event?

_____

2. What was Ahab the king of Israel's proposal (v. 4)?

_____

3. In this era the people of God had two kings. Ahab was king of Israel in the northern region. Jehoshaphat was king of Judah in the south. How did the two kings view the project differently?

_____

4. What was hard about the job of Micaiah the prophet?

_____

5. Look again at Micaiah's statements in verses 17-23. Why do you think that Ahab was an easy prey for the lying prophets?

_____

6. What did it cost Micaiah to speak God's truth?

_____

7. Why do you sometimes hesitate to say what you know to be true about God?

8. What responsibilities seem to accompany familiarity with God?

---

9. *Read 1 Kings 22:29-40.* Suppose for a moment that the events recorded here appeared on something like today's televised evening news. What might you hear and see?

What living room comments would likely ensue?

---

10. Ahab had many opportunities for hearing truth from God in the course of his life. In view of this, what do you see as the difference between hearing and receiving God's Word?

---

11. What precautions could you take to keep from acquiring Ahab's kind of deafness?

Select a paragraph from any section of the Bible. Read it aloud thoughtfully, hearing the words of your voice—and God's. Spend a few moments savoring their meaning and implications. Then respond to God in prayer.

Now or Later

Do a "walk and talk" with God. Find a favorite spot, trail, or chair. Select a section of a song or hymn. Speak aloud to God your thanks, praise, worship, and hopes as this music brings them to mind.

5

Ahaz

2 Kings 16

We had two girls, but we had planned two more children—boys, we hoped. Already, I had lost one baby in the first trimester. Pregnant again, I prayed my way through those first three months. Shortly into the second trimester the pregnancy was in trouble. We lost the baby.

And I was mad! I had done all the right things. I had been especially careful about diet, medicines, and activities. I had prayed constantly. But the baby had died inside me anyway. I prayed one angry prayer to God and then stopped praying altogether. For a while.

But God is merciful. He gave us two boys (adopted). Later I had to ask, "Why was I so mad? Is God only God for the good times? Is he a handy tool for me to get what I want and to lay aside when (in my view) he doesn't come through?" My response to trouble was not so different from that of King Ahaz. When the going got tough, Ahaz switched sides.

GROUP DISCUSSION: Why might it be hard to "keep the faith" during a dark time?

PERSONAL REFLECTION: Bring to mind one of your own dark times. Thank God for his faithfulness to you—whether or not you were able to recognize his care at that time.

King Ahaz ruled the kingdom of Judah. In a divided kingdom, these were "the good guys." But both Hebrew nations battled their mutual enemy to the north: Assyria. *Read 2 Kings 16:1-20.*

---

1. Verse 2 summarizes the reign of King Ahaz: "He did not do what was right in the eyes of the LORD his God." Review these twenty verses and find all that you can in the text that would contribute to this terse life summary for Ahaz.

---

2. In about 922 BC, God's people (the Israelites) separated into two kingdoms: Judah, where Ahaz ruled, became the southern kingdom. The other ten tribes became the northern kingdom, which was about to be swallowed up by surrounding Canaanite nations, culture, and religions. Not surprisingly the two kingdoms went to war. (Use your map on page **9** to picture this division.) What military crisis did King Ahaz face (vv. 5-6)?

---

3. What kinds of connections did Ahaz make with neighboring Assyria (vv. 7-14)?

---

4. List some of the changes Ahaz made in the temple (vv.15-18?)

5. What do Ahaz's changes within the temple suggest about his spiritual and political loyalties?

---

6. In view of the changes Ahaz made in temple furnishings and worship, what spiritual changes might you expect in the next generation of Hebrew people?

---

7. Why do you think that Ahaz said in verse 15 that he would continue to use the bronze altar "for seeking guidance"?

---

8. Think of difficult times you have experienced (e.g. a failed exam, a strong disagreement within your church, the death of someone you have prayed for, a lost relationship, unemployment, family or friends going through a divorce). What are some negative ways you have responded to such situations?

---

9. In what ways might your response to trouble sometimes become (like King Ahaz) a search for other gods and other altars?

10. How might you begin to respond to trouble in a way that builds a determined faith in God?

---

11. Much of our worship can become, like Ahaz's—an attempt to get what we want out of God. When this occurs, we need to ask ourselves, *Who is my god: God or me?* How can you make your worship less self-centered and more God-focused?

For this moment speak only thanks and praise to God based on his actions and character. Save your petitions for some later time.

Now or Later

Do a little research and review. Find a chart or listing of the kings of Judah and of Israel beginning with King Saul in about 1020 BC and ending with Zedekiah in 587. (John Bright's *A History of Israel* provides one example.) Try to recall a small fact or characteristic about as many of these ancient kings as you are able.

6

Hoshea

We had just bought a new house, a three-bedroom ranch on an acre of land. I could plant fruit trees and a vegetable garden. Our children could run and yell without disturbing neighbors. Our kitchen was big enough for two people to work together, and all six of us could sit down at the table. Best of all, there were windows everywhere. When my brother visited, he asked matter-of-factly, "Is this house your goal in life?" He meant, "Do you plan to stay here, or are you planning to 'move up'?"

I knew what he meant, but I chose to answer what he actually asked. "No, of course not," I said stoutly. "I don't think any house could be my goal in life." I could answer with confidence because I'm just not a house person, as my grubby kitchen floor and cluttered linen closet will testify. But had my brother chosen another topic (such as work, friends, family, church), I might have had to squirm. Idolatry is insidious to us all.

GROUP DISCUSSION. How might you define the difference between healthy goal setting and allowing one of your goals to take God's place?

PERSONAL REFLECTION. Why is God offended by idolatry?

King Saul stood as the first king of Israel in about 1020 BC. Nearly three hundred years later, King Hoshea held the dubious honor as Israel's last king. *Read 2 Kings 17.*

1. After studying some three-hundred years of Israel as a king-led nation, what do you find disappointing in this chapter?

2. Notice the people and places in verses 1-6. How do these verses outline the final steps to Israel's death as a nation?

3. Why was the Assyrian technique of conquering an effective way to wipe out a nation (vv. 1-6, 24)?

4. Review the list of sins (there are about twenty) in verses 7-22. What common characteristics do you find?

5. How would you summarize Israel's sin in one sentence?

6. The writer of 2 Kings says repeatedly of Israel, "The LORD removed them from his presence." Consider the events of this chapter. What did it mean to Israel in practical terms to be removed from the presence of God (vv. 18, 20, 23)?

7. Notice the references to Judah, Israel's sister nation to the south. If you had been living in Judah at the time of the events recorded here, what might you have learned about the relationship of God to his chosen people?

---

8. Why did Israel find it hard to serve one God alone (vv. 14-17)?

Why did the new Samaritans find it so hard (vv. 24-33)?

---

9. We too are vulnerable to serving "other gods." Take a private inventory of your own temptations by completing the following statements:

- I couldn't live without . . .
- When my mind is idle, it automatically turns to . . .
- If I could have anything in the world, I would choose . . .
- The most important thing (or person) to me is . . .
- I know God wants me to _____, but I can't.

In view of your inventory, in what areas of your life do you need to be alert to the temptation of idolatry?

---

10. What steps can you take to keep normal healthy interests in the world around you from turning into idolatry?

Ask God to reveal to you any priorities you have allowed to take highest place in your life. If you are able, place them under his rule and exercise your time and attention accordingly.

Now or Later

Mentally explore how you might exercise godly leadership in your own areas of responsibility in your church or civil government. Consider also how you might encourage your current civil leaders to make God-pleasing decisions.

7

Hezekiah

Taunts? With two sons less than a year apart, I've heard my share of taunts. Two boys crouch over small toy cars that zoom down newly created roads in the dirt. But this peaceful scene is too often interrupted by

"Hey! Quit muckin' up my road!"

"It's not your road. I made it."

"Well, my car's on it, so it's *my* road."

"Hey, that's not your car; it's *mine*. See—mine had the wobbly front wheel."

"My wheel got wobbly too. Hey, get your knee out of the road. You're wreckin' it. Dad!"

"Dad's not gonna do anything. I'll tell him you took my car. Dad!"

Small issues. Small children, each convinced that Dad will take his side. But when nations play such taunting games, thousands of lives are at stake. And when one king says to another, "God's not going to help you; he's on my side," a whole nation may go into crisis.

GROUP DISCUSSION. When have you thought, at least for a few moments, *God is on my side!*

Or perhaps the opposite?

PERSONAL REFECTION. What is one of your typical ways of dealing with crisis?

Because this account of Hezekiah's reign is unusually long, try reading it aloud as a drama. As much as you able, reflect with your voice the taunting in the threats, the urgency of the messengers, the fervor of the prayers. *Read 2 Kings 19:9-37.*

---

1. Sennacherib, King of Assyria, sent a message to Hezekiah, King of Judah. How was this message both a military and a religious threat?

---

2. What do you admire about the way Hezekiah handled the threat from Assyria?

---

3. What does the prayer of verses 14-19 suggest Hezekiah believed about God?

---

4. The great prophet Isaiah ministered to Judah throughout the reign of King Hezekiah. Focus on Isaiah's prophecy of verses 20-34, which begins with reassurance to Hezekiah: "I have heard your prayer . . ." What might these words have meant to a beleaguered king?

5. In your best "voice of God" tones, try reading aloud God's words to Sennacherib as recorded in verses 21-28. What can you know about your God from this message?

---

6. Review God's words to his servant Hezekiah as recorded in verses 20-34. What could Hezekiah know about the future of his troubled nation?

---

7. Verses 35-37 record the somber close of Sennecherib's attempted attack on Jerusalem. Reflect a few momemts on this text with appropriate respect for our God is the "Almighty." What did you sense in your reflection?

---

8. *Read 2 Kings 20:1-11.* King Hezekiah had the benefit of the great prophet Isaiah as his spiritual adviser during his near-fatal illness. What might Isaiah have found difficult about his physical and spiritual tasks during this crisis?

9. If you were to experience a similar brush with death, what spiritual insights would you hope to gain?

---

10. *Read 2 Kings 20:12-21.* Would you evaluate Hezekiah's actions of verses 12-19 as wise or unwise? Why?

---

11. Review the opening historical account of Hezekiah's reign as summarized in 2 Kings 18:1-3. What elements of God's grace do you see in that summary?

---

12. When and how have you experienced God's grace?

Enter a time of prayer with silent reflection. When and under what circumstances have you received grace from God? In the presence of God, reflect on his grace and give thanks.

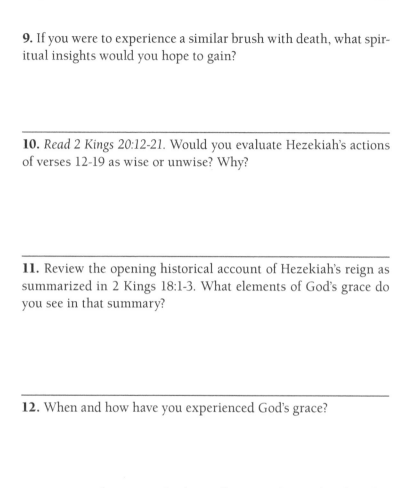

Now or Later

As prayer, reflection, and testimony of God's grace, read, sing, or pray this hymn written by Joseph Scriven in about 1855.

What a Friend we have in Jesus, all our sins and griefs to bear!
What a privilege to carry everything to God in prayer!

O what peace we often forfeit, O what needless pain we bear,
All because we do not carry everything to God in prayer!

Have we trials and temptations? Is there trouble anywhere?
We should never be discouraged; take it to the Lord in
        prayer!
Can we find a friend so faithful who will all our sorrows
        share?
Jesus knows our every weakness; take it to the Lord in prayer!

Are we weak and heavy laden, cumbered with a load of care?
Precious Savior, still our refuge—take it to the Lord in
        prayer!
Do thy friends despise, forsake thee? Take it to the Lord in
        prayer!
In his arms he'll take and shield thee; thou wilt find a
        solace there.

8

Manasseh

My friends Bob and Dottie and their children were missionaries to a primitive tribe in South America. After some initial awkwardness, they were well-received. They donned the long white tunics of the tribal people, carried their woven handbags, and wore many necklaces of tiny beads. They washed clothing native style by beating them on the riverside rocks. They carried their babies like papooses (it was easier for climbing mountains). They ate local food—caught or grown.

The indigenous people helped Bob and Dottie learn their language and regularly appeared at their door for medical help when they were sick or wounded. To my friends, God seemed ready to bring these people into his kingdom.

Then drug traffic swept the area. Speculators bought the land or massacred owners who were reluctant to sell. Twentieth-century viruses, previously unknown to this isolated people group, decimated the tribe. Bob and his young son were falsely accused, arrested, and jailed. The area had become too dangerous for mission work. In fact, only two-thirds of the native population remained alive. And some who were left looked at my friends with hostile eyes.

Can we still trust God when all the trends run counter to what we know of his purposes? One of the advantages of studying the Old Testament is seeing, in only a few pages, God moving through hundreds of years of history. It may help us trust God's unseen purposes for our own small part.

GROUP DISCUSSION. What cultural trends in your own setting seem to go against God's standard of what is right?

PERSONAL REFLECTION. As you look back on your own life, what has been one of your most spiritually difficult eras?

As had been the norm for more than three hundred years in the nation of Judah, a son succeeded his father to the throne. Thus, ready or not, Manasseh became king and reigned for fifty-five years. *Read 2 Kings 21:1-18.*

---

1. Focus on verses 1-9. When you envision life in Judah under Manasseh, a boy-king born to the great reformer Hezekiah in his old age and reigning as king for more than five decades, what pictures come to your mind?

---

2. If you were attempting to raise a God-honoring family during Manasseh's rule, what hardships might you need to overcome?

---

3. Reread verse 8 with its promise, along with the conditions of that promise. If you were headed home after a first visit to your temple now refurbished by Manasseh, what might you do when you got home?

4. Verse 12 begins with the stern voice of God: "This is what the LORD, the God of Israel, says . . ." What did God promise?

_____

5. What do the symbols of a measuring line, plumb line, and dish reveal about Judah's future (see vv. 12-15)?

_____

6. What sobering information do verses 10-16 reveal of God's nature?

_____

7. Suppose you were living in Judah at this time. If you heard this prophecy of 2 Kings 21:12-15 and believed it to be true, what would you do?

_____

8. There is no Old Testament prophet who claims to have written during Manasseh's reign. Why do you think this is the case?

_____

9. *Read 2 Kings 21:19-26.* The entire reign of King Amon (son of Manasseh) is recorded in a mere eight verses of 2 Kings 21:19-26. What similarities and differences do you see in how this father and son worshiped and ruled?

10. Review Hezekiah's situation in 2 Kings 20:1-11. If Hezekiah could have known the future, including the birth of his son, do you think he would have wanted God to add fifteen years to his life? Why or why not?

_____

11. What do you know about God that might encourage you to resist current trends in your own culture that go against what you know is right?

_____

12. How can you serve God in your response to these trends?

Read the latest newspaper and let your eyes wander from one article to another. Pray about what you find there.

Now or Later

Educate yourself about your own local government. How might you assist in creating better government within your local system? Send a thank you note to one government leader you respect.

9

Josiah

2 Kings 22:1–23:30

Seniors in high school typically get a little huffy about restrictive school rules such as hall passes and washroom permits. Sometimes even teachers are not immune to similar feelings. When my daughter's music teacher, accustomed to working with diligent honors students, was confronted with the request for one more hall pass for an in-building errand, he wrote, "Sheri has my permission to be in the hall so that she can check the drug supply in her locker. Antonia is her bodyguard." (They weren't stopped.)

There's something inside us that grates against laws—of any kind—unless, of course, we've had to live a long time without them. Judah had such an experience.

GROUP DISCUSSION. What rules annoyed you during your own teen years?

PERSONAL REFLECTION. What are some of your own mixed feelings about laws?

Manasseh and his son Amnon had ruled in Judah for a total of forty-four years, from about 686–640 BC. During that time the nation of Judah adopted the pagan religions of neighboring nations: multiple gods for multiple occasions—each one an object to be used, manipulated, appeased, and sometimes revered. King Amnon, son of the evil Manasseh, ruled as king of Judah for a mere two years and then died, assassinated by his own officials. And Josiah, his eight-year-old grandson, stepped up to the throne. *Read 2 Kings 22:1–23:30.*

---

1. What steps led to finding the Book of the Law (22:1-8)?

---

2. What can you know about Huldah (22:14-20)?

---

3. What could Josiah know about God from her message?

---

4. What effect would you expect the scene in 2 Kings 23:1-3 to have on the people?

---

5. *Read 2 Kings 23:4-30.* These verses list some sixteen religious reforms that Josiah instituted. As you read through these reforms, what do you learn about the spiritual practices of the people before Josiah became king?

6. How would you expect the life of an ordinary person to be affected by these changes?

_____

7. Much of today's culture ignores God's laws. What pressures do you feel to follow the culture rather than the law of God?

_____

8. In what different ways did Josiah show respect for the law of God? (Draw from all of 2 Kings 22–23.)

_____

9. What words and phrases describe Josiah in 2 Kings 23:25?

_____

10. What relationship do you see between our response to God's law and our concept of God?

_____

11. Study more carefully the words in 2 Kings 23:25 describing Josiah's commitment to God and to God's law. What aspect of that description would you like to make a greater part of your own commitment?

12. God's law is tied to his character. As you think of your own natural resistance to law, what steps could you take to bring your response to God's law in line with what you believe to be true of God?

Pray, focusing on God's nature, his character, his work, his love.

Now or Later

If you are a lover of history, you might want a friendly chat with the writer of this study guide when you come to this section of the Kings. "You left out three kings!" might be your opening complaint.

"Yes I did," comes the reply. History lovers will have already consulted John Bright's charts in his *A History of Israel* and spotted the missing era of 609–597 BC. They will also have read the biblical (and depressing) texts of 2 Kings 23:31–24:17, with its minimal accounts of each of these three kings. Jehoahaz (three months reign), Jehoiakim (eleven years or so), and his son Jehoiachin for a final three months, who then surrendered himself and his family, along with any remaining gold in the temple. Babylonian forces carted him away as their prisoner. Depressing readings of those twelve years or so before Judah's final king ended the kingly line.

Try shifting from reader to artist as you contemplate this era of the nation of Judah recorded in 2 Kings 23:31–24:17. Read the text aloud—as a lament. Then illustrate the text in some nonverbal way: a pencil sketch, chalk drawing, chart, cartoon, abstract painting, or musical chant. If you are meeting with a group, bring your creation to your next meeting.

10

Zedekiah

2 Kings 24:1–25:21

Dig you prophet, Dig in the wall
Probe the hole that opens to the night
Weep Ezekiel, Weep for your call

Crumble small the whitewash with your awl
Daubed by holy priests who smothered light
Dig you prophet, Dig in the wall

Dig you deeper, Dig back to the fall
Hasten shepherd, see your flock's in flight
Weep Ezekiel, Weep for your call

Hide your eyes and shrink from the small
Door that dries your bones as if you might
Not dig. You watchman, Dig in the wall

Seventy elders, sentries of God's law
Worship beasts and creatures slimed with blight
Weep Ezekiel, Weep for your call

Watch the Spirit flee among the tall
Cherubim, who bear Him out of sight
Hear the curse of God upon your wall
Weep you watchman, Weep for your call*

---

* Carolyn Nystrom, "Ezekiel 8," 1980.

GROUP DISCUSSION. The prophet Ezekiel held the responsibility as prophet of the living God during the final years before much of the Hebrew population was herded off to exile in Babylon. What do you know about God that might comfort you at such a time?

PERSONAL REFLECTION. Read the biblical chapter of Ezekiel 8. Write a few words of your own lament as if you are one of the few remaining faithful in this era of Israel's history.

In this final section of Judah's history of a nation, the amount of loss is difficult to comprehend. *Read 2 Kings 24:1–25:21.*

1. What do you find painful in this reading?

2. Using the material you've read in these last two chapters of the Kings, trace the final steps of the nation of Judah.

3. What events in those final years make the strongest impression on your mind?

Why do these events seem especially haunting?

4. Look more carefully at 2 Kings 24:3-4 and 20. What cautions might these words bring to your own life?

5. Consider the history of Israel and Judah. What turning points do you see that led to this kind of end?

---

6. How might this study of Jewish history affect the way you pray for your own nation and its leaders?

---

7. For what specific national needs or leaders should you be praying?

---

8. Focus on the final scene of Judah's kings in 2 Kings 25:27-30. Would you say that this is good news or bad news for the people of God? Why?

---

9. What spiritual temptations would Jehoiachin, king of Judah, deal with in his Babylonian setting?

---

10. In your own experience have you found periods of hardship or of ease most conducive to deepening your faith? How and why, and with what lasting results?

Thank God for his teachings and for his patience with these ancient people he called his own. Thank him for your own small place in the company called "the people of God."

Now or Later

During the time that Zedekiah and his people were about to be deported to Babylon, the prophet Jeremiah wrote a letter to the Hebrew people already captive in Babylon. Review God's words to them in Jeremiah 29:10-13.

If you had been a Hebrew captive in Babylon, what effect might these words have on the way you conducted your life during your captivity?

What does the prophet Jeremiah reveal about the character of God?

What personal hope do these words from Jeremiah offer to you?

Leader's Notes

MY GRACE IS SUFFICIENT FOR YOU. (2 CORINTHIANS 12:9)

Leading a Bible discussion can be an enjoyable and rewarding experience. But it can also be *scary*—especially if you've never done it before. If this is your feeling, you're in good company. When God asked Moses to lead the Israelites out of Egypt, he replied, "Please send someone else" (Exodus 4:13)! It was the same with Solomon, Jeremiah, and Timothy, but God helped these people in spite of their weaknesses, and he will help you as well.

You don't need to be an expert on the Bible or a trained teacher to lead a Bible discussion. The idea behind these inductive studies is that the leader guides group members to discover for themselves what the Bible has to say. This method of learning will allow group members to remember much more of what is said than a lecture would.

These studies are designed to be led easily. As a matter of fact, the flow of questions through the passage from observation to interpretation to application is so natural that you may feel that the studies lead themselves. This study guide is also flexible. You can use it with a variety of groups—student, professional, neighborhood, or church groups. Each study takes forty-five to sixty minutes in a group setting.

There are some important facts to know about group dynamics and encouraging discussion. The suggestions listed below should enable you to effectively and enjoyably fulfill your role as leader.

Preparing for the Study

1. Ask God to help you understand and apply the passage in your own life. Unless this happens, you will not be prepared to lead others. Pray too for the various members of the group. Ask God to open your hearts to the message of his Word and motivate you to action.

2. Read the introduction to the guide to get an overview of the entire book and the issues that will be explored.

3. As you begin each study, read and reread the assigned Bible passage to familiarize yourself with it.

4. This study guide is based on the New International Version of the Bible. It will help you and the group if you use this translation as the basis for your study and discussion.

5. Carefully work through each question in the study. Spend time in meditation and reflection as you consider how to respond.

6. Write your thoughts and responses in the space provided in the study guide. This will help you to express your understanding of the passage clearly.

7. It might help to have a Bible dictionary handy. Use it to look up any unfamiliar words, names, or places. (For additional help on how to study a passage, see chapter five of *How to Lead a LifeBuilder Bible Study,* IVP, 2018.)

8. Consider how you can apply the Scripture to your life. Remember that the group will follow your lead in responding to the studies. They will not go any deeper than you do.

9. Once you have finished your own study of the passage, familiarize yourself with the leader's notes for the study you are leading. These are designed to help you in several ways. First, they tell you the purpose the study guide author had in mind when writing the study. Take time to think through how the study questions work together to accomplish that purpose. Second, the notes provide you with additional background information or suggestions on group dynamics for various questions. This information can be useful when people have difficulty understanding or answering a question. Third, the leader's notes can alert you to potential problems you may encounter during the study.

10. If you wish to remind yourself of anything mentioned in the leader's notes, make a note to yourself below that question in the study.

Leading the Study

1. Begin the study on time. Open with prayer, asking God to help the group to understand and apply the passage.

2. Be sure that everyone in your group has a study guide. Encourage the group to prepare beforehand for each discussion by reading the introduction to the guide and by working through the questions in the study.

3. At the beginning of your first time together, explain that these studies are meant to be discussions, not lectures. Encourage the members of the group to participate. However, do not put pressure on those who may be hesitant to speak during the first few sessions. You may want to suggest the following guidelines to your group.

☐ Stick to the topic being discussed.

☐ Your responses should be based on the verses that are the focus of the discussion and not on outside authorities such as commentaries or speakers.

☐ These studies focus on a particular passage of Scripture. Only rarely should you refer to other portions of the Bible. This allows for everyone to participate in in-depth study on equal ground.

☐ Anything said in the group is considered confidential and will not be discussed outside the group unless specific permission is given to do so.

☐ We will listen attentively to each other and provide time for each person present to talk.

☐ We will pray for each other.

4. Have a group member read the introduction at the beginning of the discussion.

5. Every session begins with a group discussion question. The question or activity is meant to be used before the passage is read. The question introduces the theme of the study and encourages group members to begin to open up. Encourage as many members as possible to participate, and be ready to get the discussion going with your own response.

This section is designed to reveal where our thoughts or feelings need to be transformed by Scripture. That is why it is especially important not to read the passage before the discussion question is asked. The passage will tend to color the honest reactions people would otherwise give because they are, of course, supposed to think the way the Bible does.

You may want to supplement the group discussion question with an icebreaker to help people get comfortable. See the community section of the *Small Group Starter Kit* (IVP, 1995) for more ideas.

You also might want to use the personal reflection question with your group. Either allow a time of silence for people to respond individually or discuss it together.

6. Have a group member (or members if the passage is long) read aloud the passage to be studied. Then give people several minutes to read the passage again silently so that they can take it all in.

7. Question 1 will generally be an overview question designed to briefly survey the passage. Encourage the group to look at the whole passage, but try to avoid getting sidetracked by questions or issues that will be addressed later in the study.

8. As you ask the questions, keep in mind that they are designed to be used just as they are written. You may simply read them aloud. Or you may prefer to express them in your own words.

There may be times when it is appropriate to deviate from the study guide. For example, a question may have already been answered. If so, move on to the next question. Or someone may raise an important question not covered in the guide. Take time to discuss it, but try to keep the group from going off on tangents.

9. Avoid answering your own questions. If necessary, repeat or rephrase them until they are clearly understood. Or point out something you read in the leader's notes to clarify the context or meaning. An eager group quickly becomes passive and silent if they think the leader will do most of the talking.

10. Don't be afraid of silence. People may need time to think about the question before formulating their answers.

11. Don't be content with just one answer. Ask, "What do the rest of you think?" or "Anything else?" until several people have given answers to the question.

12. Acknowledge all contributions. Try to be affirming whenever possible. Never reject an answer. If it is clearly off-base, ask,

"Which verse led you to that conclusion?" or again, "What do the rest of you think?"

13. Don't expect every answer to be addressed to you, even though this will probably happen at first. As group members become more at ease, they will begin to truly interact with each other. This is one sign of healthy discussion.

14. Don't be afraid of controversy. It can be very stimulating. If you don't resolve an issue completely, don't be frustrated. Move on and keep it in mind for later. A subsequent study may solve the problem.

15. Periodically summarize what the group has said about the passage. This helps to draw together the various ideas mentioned and gives continuity to the study. But don't preach.

16. At the end of the Bible discussion you may want to allow group members a time of quiet to work on an idea under "Now or Later." Then discuss what you experienced. Or you may want to encourage group members to work on these ideas between meetings. Give an opportunity during the session for people to talk about what they are learning.

17. Conclude your time together with conversational prayer, adapting the prayer suggestion at the end of the study to your group. Ask for God's help in following through on the commitments you've made.

18. End on time.

Many more suggestions and helps are found in *How to Lead a LifeBuilder Bible Study.*

Components of Small Groups
A healthy small group should do more than study the Bible. There are four components to consider as you structure your time together.

Nurture. Small groups help us to grow in our knowledge and love of God. Bible study is the key to making this happen and is the foundation of your small group.

Community. Small groups are a great place to develop deep friendships with other Christians. Allow time for informal interaction before and after each study. Plan activities and games that will help you get to know each other. Spend time having fun together going on a picnic or cooking dinner together.

Worship and prayer. Your study will be enhanced by spending time praising God together in prayer or song. Pray for each other's needs and keep track of how God is answering prayer in your group. Ask God to help you to apply what you are learning in your study.

Outreach. Reaching out to others can be a practical way of applying what you are learning, and it will keep your group from becoming self-focused. Host a series of evangelistic discussions for your friends or neighbors. Clean up the yard of an elderly friend. Serve at a soup kitchen together, or spend a day working in the community.

Many more suggestions and helps in each of these areas are found in the *Small Group Starter Kit.* You will also find information on building a small group. Reading through the starter kit will be worth your time.

Before each study, you may want to put an asterisk by the key questions you think are most important for your group to cover, in case you don't have time to cover all the questions. As we suggested in "Getting the Most Out of *1 & 2 Kings*," if you want to make sure you have enough time to discuss all the questions, you have other options. For example, the group could decide to extend each meeting to ninety minutes or more. Alternatively, you could devote two sixty-minute sessions to each study.

Study 1. Solomon: Praying with God's Values. 1 Kings 3.
Purpose: To learn to pray effectively in ways pleasing to God.
Group discussion. Try to involve each person with this question. Draw on personal experience, acquaintances, or even reports in the media. The object is to help the group appreciate the value of shared prayer.
Personal reflection. These questions are designed for individuals studying on their own. However, they also work well in a group if people are allowed a few minutes of silence to reflect on them as

they prepare for study. Guard your group's time at the opening so that you can complete the entire study in your allotted time. Closing questions are often more important than openings because the final questions allow understanding of the biblical text to shape patterns of life.

Questions 1-2. If your group wishes to evaluate some of Solomon's early actions, refer them momentarily to Deuteronomy 12:1-7, then quickly return to the text of 1 Kings 3.

Question 3. Key words and phrases include *servant* (vv. 7, 8, 9), *little child* (v. 7), *duties* (v. 7), LORD *my God* (v. 7), *great people* (v. 8), *chosen* (v. 8), and *people of yours* (v. 9).

Note: Though Solomon uses the term *little child* in verse 7, he was probably speaking metaphorically. In the year 971 BC, an estimated beginning of his reign, he was likely a young adult in his early twenties.

Questions 4-5. The biblical text offers such gifts as riches, honor, wealth, discernment, and even "long life" with an accompanying "if you walk in obedience to me . . ."

Question 10. Your group might speculate on the possible outcome if both women had protested the slaughter, if neither had, or if the wrong woman had protested.

Question 12. Encourage people to mention specific and concrete actions that would lead in that direction. Be sure to include prayers of worship and confession as well as prayers of petition. After Solomon asked (correctly) of God, he worshiped and made a sacrifice.

Keep your prayers brief. People may pray more than once if they want. Allow time for everyone to add something to these sentence prayers.

Study 2. Solomon: Faithless in Love. 1 Kings 11.

Purpose: To make our love for God even more important than our love for any person.

Question 6. Refer, if necessary, to Exodus 20:3. God gives us, as a precious gift, the beauty of human love. Even so, he demands that we give our highest allegiance to him alone. Help your group discuss ways to enjoy this human love (within its proper limits) but still keep God first.

Question 8. Notice that God had already given this message to Solomon (vv. 11-13). A question about the number of tribes may arise. Ten plus one did not equal twelve by the math in Solomon's time either! The *New Bible Commentary* suggests that the tribe of Judah eventually absorbed the nearby tribe of Benjamin. Therefore, Solomon was to lose the northern ten tribes but retain the southern two tribes that eventually became one tribe—Judah.

Question 9. Notice the promises God makes in verses 35 and 37, and the conditions in verse 38.

Question 10. Idolatry, intermarriage, rebellion, and self-centeredness are some of the sins that might have been root causes of Solomon's spiritual fall.

Question 11. Confession is always hard, so don't expect graphic details. Encourage several people to mention at least one general area in which they sense that God is convicting them.

Study 3. Jeroboam and Rehoboam. 1 Kings 12.

Purpose: To worship God in spite of conflict within our worship groups.

Question 1. Answers should be detailed and in sequence. Citing verse numbers will help the group to stay together. Someone should point out where the two leaders were at the beginning of the chapter and why. But don't spend more than a tenth of your discussion time on this question.

Question 2. In defense of Rehoboam's harsh answer, the proper place for inauguration was Jerusalem. Yet Rehoboam went to Shechem in the north, probably because the people there would not come south to Jerusalem. Notice Jeroboam's swift return from exile in Egypt—a hostile signal to Rehoboam. Notice also Adoniram, his position, and his death.

Question 5. Verse 15 refers to 1 Kings 11:30-31. The events of verses 22-24 prevented unnecessary bloodshed.

Question 7. Jeroboam set up two worship sites: Bethel and Dan were on the way to Jerusalem for people traveling on foot from the north. The golden calf positioned in Bethel reminded travelers of idols their ancestors worshiped on their way out of Egypt, and might be a "sight worth seeing" (see Exodus 32). But the convenience and the calves drew the people to idolatry and away from the true living God who had prescribed worship in Jerusalem. Their civil war thus became also a spiritual war—with three cities as magnets to false gods.

Question 8. These two places of false worship (Bethel and Dan) appear again and again throughout the next two hundred years of Jewish history. They eventually become a partial cause for the separation of the Jews of Judah and a people later called the Samaritans.

Question 10. This question assumes some knowledge of the law as given in Exodus and Deuteronomy. Find several ways in which Jeroboam disobeyed God in these verses.

Question 12. Frequency of church attendance is only one area to discuss. Think also about the ways you use opportunities for fellowship with other believers. (Do you fight over petty issues when you should be enjoying oneness in Christ?) And what do you actually do and think during worship—in public as well as in private?

Question 13. Use this question to encourage several group members to plan more effective use of their opportunities to worship.

Study 4. Ahab. 1 Kings 22:1-40.
Purpose: To act on what we know of God and thereby resist spiritual deafness.

Question 1. Your character list should include Ahab, Jehoshaphat, Zedekiah, a messenger, 400 prophets, Micaiah and the Lord.

Question 3. Find Ramoth Gilead on your map. Notice that it was on or near a major trade route. Verse 2 reads, "Jehoshaphat . . . went down to see the king of Israel." Here, as throughout Kings and Chronicles, people travel down from Jerusalem—even if they are headed north. This is because Jerusalem is at a high elevation. To travel anywhere is down.

Question 4. For background on the relationship between Israel and Aram (Syria), review quickly 1 Kings 20. Note particularly the terms of the treaty between Ahab and Ben-Hadad (1 Kings 20:34). If you are leading a group, briefly summarize your findings.

Question 6. If your group has trouble coming to the point, re-phrase the question to ask, "What do these words reveal about God's purposes in these events?" They should notice that God was in control, even of the lying prophets. And that God had deter-mined to send Ahab to his death by this means. See especially verses 13-14, 24 and 26-27.

Question 10-11. These questions begin to move the discussion into a twentieth-century framework. Pace your study so that about ten minutes remain for these application questions.

Study 5. Ahaz. 2 Kings 16.

Purpose: To trust God—even when he does not give us what we want.

Question 1. Almost every sentence of the text contributes to the wrongness of Ahaz's reign. Highlight particularly the several ways he detracted or distracted from worship of the God by adopting and adapting worship of local pagan gods. He "even sacrificed his son in the fire," a particularly brutal form of pagan worship.

Question 2. Judah, the Southern kingdom, kept more or less faithful to God. The remaining ten tribes, the Northern king-dom, became more and more like their Canaanite neighbors. On the map, notice that Elath was Judah's most Southern city, which extended the influence of Ahaz (king of the North) about as far south into Judah as possible. A potential confusion comes in verse 5, where Remalia, king of Israel, marched *up* to Jerusalem. You will notice on the map, however, that Israel, where Remalia ruled, is the Northern kingdom. Yet Jerusalem was in Judah, the South-ern kingdom. The answer to this confusion again lies in elevation. Because Jerusalem was at the top of a high hill, everyone traveled *up* to Jerusalem.

Question 3. Check the map for changes in the Assyrian borders. By forming an alliance with the most dangerous nation in the area, Ahaz had brought Assyrian borders to his own doorstep. Group members should also notice, in verse 9, the treatment a conquered nation could expect from Assyria. Ahaz had also been guilty, before God, of turning his sister nation (Israel) over to a common enemy. Participants may find other reasons that grow out of this passage.

Question 4. See 1 Chronicles 28:19-21 for more information about the instructions God gave to David regarding building and furnishing God's temple.

Questions 5. For more details about this same event under the rule of King Ahaz, read Isaiah 7:1-14. Embedded in this rather sorry story of a Hebrew king, you will find surprise: a portent of Christ's birth.

Question 9. Group members should respond to these questions in a way that fits their own troublesome situations. Possible attempts to find "other gods and other altars" in the sample situations might include "I would leave my church that is in turmoil"; "I would stop praying for a while when my friend dies"; "I would express excessive anger at my spouse, assuming he or she, not God, is to take care of me"; "I would put *all* my faith in counseling as an aid to my friends who are getting divorced, not putting counseling in its proper perspective as one of the gifts from a living God who hates divorce."

Study 6. Hoshea. 2 Kings 17.
Purpose: To examine our lives for temptation toward idolatry.

Question 1. Invite everyone present to answer this question in some way. Ask several to explain why they feel the way they do.

Question 2. Someone may point out the apparent time discrepancy between 2 Kings 15:30 and 17:1. In their *Old Testament Commentaries*, Carl F. Keil and Franz Delitzsch explain this by suggesting that in this turbulent era an eight-year period of anarchy probably occurred before Hoshea was able to secure the throne (*First Kings–Esther* [Grand Rapids: Eerdmans, 1971], 4:409).

Question 3. Notice the details of verses 1-6 as well as verse 24. Along with the other details, notice that Assyria imprisoned the Israeli king, captured the people of Israel, deported them to a land some six hundred miles away, and spread out the Jews so they could not form a cohesive group. At the same time, to make sure there would be no vacant land to invite a return, Assyria imported other peoples to Samaria and settled them there. Second Chronicles 30:5-11 and 2 Chronicles 34:6-9 suggest that a few Jews escaped deportation, but even these must have mingled with the imported groups and lost any Jewish identity.

It might be helpful to clarify at this point that while Hoshea presided as king over the final years of Israel's existence, the Southern kingdom of God's people (Judah) remained in existence for another 135 years until 587 BC. Thus you will continue to study the kings—but the remaining kings will be rulers from this Southern kingdom, originally composed of descendants of Jacob's son Judah and likely also the descendants of Levi, from whom the priests descended.

Question 8. Numerous factors influenced the people of Israel and the newly formed Samaritans toward idolatry. Find a dozen or so factors in verses 14-17 and verses 24-33.

Questions 9-10. Save at least ten minutes for these final application questions. Encourage several group members to respond as honestly as is practical. After others have spoken, be ready to share some of your own thinking on the subject.

In all of history, we never again see this nation. In fact, it is often called "the ten lost tribes."

Study 7. Hezekiah. 2 Kings 19:9–20:21.
Purpose: In crisis, turn to God—not away from him.

Question 1. Details here will outline much of the text—and the painful era ahead for a people that God had called to be his own.

Question 3. Even though Hezekiah and his nation were in dire straits, Hezekiah's prayer is full of worship. Approach the text phrase by phrase, then take time to meditate on God's character as it is revealed in this cry for help.

Question 6. This prophecy of Isaiah recorded in 2 Kings 19:20-34 covers a fair amount of text in graphic language and poetic tones as it proclaims the power of the God of the Hebrews—a power about to be exercised in favor of the nation of Judah's and against its surrounding enemies, including King Sennacherib of the Assyrians. Spend enough time with it to savor various levels of understanding and the God who proclaims himself in this way.

Question 8. Use this question to put yourself in Isaiah's sandals as he intercedes between a holy and almighty God and the rather shortsighted leaders of God's chosen people.

Question 11-12. Christians often think of God's grace as a New Testament concept given through Jesus Christ—the Son of the living God. But God's nature is grace (as well as truth and righteousness). We can draw on God's identity with and among and on behalf of his people as we track his work among Hebrew kings, many of doubtful ability and dubious or inaccurate faith. Yet God himself is faithful—an aspect of his grace.

Christians of our current era have experienced that grace through the redeeming work of Jesus Christ. We walk spiritually with him as God, our Friend. We can look forward to sharing eternity of shared faith with our God-following, Christ-anticipating friends from the Old Testament: kings, prophets, common folk. Friends of God.

Study 8. Manasseh. 2 Kings 21:1-26.

Purpose: To develop a faith that can endure a spiritually unfriendly environment.

Question 1. Let these first nine verses of history inform your thinking. When you envision life in Judah under Manasseh, what probable events come to your mind? Some may ask what the text means when it says, "He sacrificed his own son in the fire" (v. 6). Judah's neighboring pagans did sometimes offer fatal child sacrifices to their gods. However, some translations use the phrase "He made his son pass through the fire" (e.g., KJV, NASB, NRSV), which suggests that what Manasseh did may not have been fatal, though it certainly was damaging. And certainly idolatrous.

Question 6. C. S. Lewis captured some of God's character in *The Lion, the Witch, and the Wardrobe* when Aslan disappeared from their closing celebration and Mr. Beaver informed the disappointed Lucy, "He's wild you know. Not like a *tame* lion." The God of mercy and love and kindness and grace is also a God of wrath. In the closing years of their kingdom, the people of Israel earned (and experienced) that wrath.

Spend enough time with verses 8-15 to appreciate the graphic language of God's anger and how his people might have experienced the results of his wrath. Even the rumor of forcing a child to "pass through fire" would keep many parents from entering their place of worship. And their temple built and furnished according to God's design through the great King Solomon now contained images of all kinds of pagan deities and implements for worshiping them (vv. 4-7). This would be in direct conflict with the third command God gave through Moses some six hundred years back: "You shall not make for yourself an image in the form of anything in heaven above or the earth beneath or in the waters below. You shall not bow down to them or worship them; for I, the LORD your God, am a jealous God" (Exodus 20:4-5).

Question 7. With our New Testament hindsight, we endanger ourselves and those we teach if we entirely forget that although God is love, he is also acts in wrath. With some six hundred years of history with the people he has called his own, this generation of the mid-600s BC experienced his wrath. Of course there were righteous people among them, the prophet Isaiah, for example, along with King Hezekiah. But the nation itself was doomed. Their ungodly King Manasseh, by his own unfaithfulness (perhaps in an attempt to placate neighboring nations with different gods), would contribute to that destruction.

Question 9. A sobering silence surrounds these final years of Judah's kings. The nation existed (sort of) for another forty-five years after King Manasseh died in 642 BC. But each king ruled an increasingly weakened kingdom.

Meanwhile, across the Mediterranean Sea an artistically inclined nation named Greece, with its sculptures and philosophers, was rising to world prominence with high influence from 800–146 BC. And even further to the northwest a Mediterranean peninsula with military and governmental prowess would follow as the major world power of Rome from 146 BC to about AD 330. At its peek Rome would govern much that surrounded the great Mediterranean, even the relatively small bits of land that had encompassed both Israel's Northern and Southern kingdoms. And in that era some six centuries after King Manasseh's reign and fall, but in that same strip of troubled land, the Messiah, our Savior Jesus was born. One of his titles would be King of Kings.

Study 9. Josiah. 2 Kings 22:1–23:30.
Purpose: To practice respect for God's law.
Question 5. It is interesting to note that Hezekiah also celebrated Passover as part of his reform (see 2 Chronicles 30). But Hezekiah did not have the benefit of specific instructions for Passover from the Book of the Law. And his animal sacrifices were only one-tenth of those recorded for Josiah. Second Chronicles 35:7 states that the sacrificial animals came from Josiah's own possessions. If you want more information on "the man of God who came from Judah" in 2 Kings 23:17, read 1 Kings 13.
Question 7. If the question of New Testament law versus Old Testament law comes into the discussion in this or a later question, you could comment that Old Testament law is often divided into three categories: ceremonial law, civil law, and moral law. New Testament Christians need only be bound by the moral law of the Old Testament. But distinguishing what is moral law from the other two categories is no small task.
Question 10. If you want the discussion to take a more personal direction, ask, "Think back on your own responses to God's law. Try to think of a specific standard of behavior that you became aware of rather suddenly. What were your first feelings about that law?" For an alternate question or a followup question, ask, "Why is the term *law,* even if it belongs to God, hard for us to live with?"
Question 12. If time permits ask also, "What does the fact that God sets standards of behavior for his people reveal about the character of God?"
Now or Later. If you are leading a group, point out the homework relating to 2 Kings 23:31–24:17. Plan to open your next gathering with display of and appropriate respect for each contribution. If this is an on-your-own study for you, consider posting your creation in front of you as you work through the final study about King Zedekiah.

Study 10. Zedekiah. 2 Kings 24:1–25:21.
Purpose: To accept God's kind sovereignty over the events of history.

Question 3. Help your group tell, in sequence, the outline of events recorded here.

Question 7. If people in your group are comfortable with praying together, this might be a good time to lead a brief time of prayer for any national and world leaders who come to mind.

Question 10. Encourage a brief sentence of response from each person present.

If your group would like to telescope nearly six hundred years in time, they will find new people in the same places. Read Matthew 1:6–2:12. There you will find a list of the kings, with a few more names added at the end. And you will find God's people once again living near Jerusalem. Important visitors from the East (Babylon?) come to see a new Hebrew king. His name is Immanuel: God with us.

Carolyn Nystrom (MA, Wheaton College) has written more than eighty books, Bible study guides, and children's titles. She co-wrote Praying *with theologian J. I. Packer and Is the* Reformation Over? *with scholar Mark Noll. She is also the author of the LifeBuilder Bible Studies* 1 & 2 Peter and Jude, Money and Work, Friendship, Listening to God, *and more. In addition to actively serving in her church, she has been a foster parent, an elementary school teacher, the stated clerk of her Evangelical Presbyterian Church presbytery, and a book editor. Carolyn lives in northern Illinois with her husband; they have four grown children.*